Twelve Love Poems to Read Aloud

by

Carol Frome

Published by *795 Press*

For

_____

on the joyous occasion
of their commitment to one another

on

_____

at

_____

as Witnessed by

_____

_____

*For Everyone Who Has the Space of Heart
to Love Another for a Lifetime*

A Note on Reading Poetry Aloud

Poetry is the oldest form of literature, and it still matters to us today. We still turn to poetry to give voice to the unsayable, to the unspeakable, to grief, to mystery, and to the sublime.

Yet, most of us are unpracticed readers of poetry, particularly contemporary poetry--that of our own time.

In these poems, I worked to connect lyricism with the lived life, especially that part of it that dwells inside an enduring committed relationship.

Spoken aloud, poetry quickens with life, so I urge you to read these poems aloud to someone you love. My hope is that you will hear the poetry of your own life together resonating.

Read with emphasis and conviction, but without theatrics. If you need to, ignore the line breaks as you speak. Or pause for a slight moment at each line break. Either way, the music will emerge.

I

Not one day goes by
when I don't know
your love fleeting toward me,
declaring itself at your glance
or your touch. And sometimes,
in the very early morning,
I see it waiting as a dream,
quickening in your sleeping eyes,
that, always, I want to imagine
as your quiet dream
of our love for each other.

II

Photons are particles of light
that fly from the sun and
bombard us. They enter the eye,
which then creates more light,
its own light, ardent particles
which when I look at you
I see as love's evidence,
the very bones, blood, flesh
and muscle, the luminous heart
of your love, and of my love
seeking yours.

III

These poems I send you
I send for us, to remind us
to forget, to forget
the echoing workaday,
forget the calling tensions,
let go the faces of judgment.
And they are to remind us, also,
not to forget our hands that love each other,
not to forget our quickening arms
that reach, you for me, me for you, and love,
not to forget love, that sustenance
that nourishes our future together.

IV

Please accept this poem
as partial tender
for my room and board
in the residence of our union.
The rest of my glad debt,
I promise, you will find
growing in our garden,
a garden that couldn't thrive
if it weren't for our efforts,
but that blooms, now
fulsome with flowers and herbs,
at love's nourishing touch.

V

I arrive home knowing
you'll be there—before me,
after me—it doesn't matter,
but the knowing is always
a tenderness. It's the comfort
of preparing and seasoning
another evening's meal
with cumin, curry,
cinnamon, a little salt,
and the movement of our hands
paring apples.
It's the comfort of flavor
that we create for ourselves,
and an evening of listening
that sounds like love
murmuring the scent of apples.

VI

It's hard to care about anywhere else
but here, with you, where our fields
are honeyed with wildflowers,
even though some
are the purple eyes of thistle.
Thistle, sturdy at the root, perseveres
through drought and difficulty,
through rain and rough spots in the soil,
so among the flowers, I welcome thistle
and its purple, unwavering, loyalty,
a sign of endearment more than endurance,
as part of the mystery
of this love, our beauty.

VII

I wanted you before I knew you,
but I had to learn patience, learn
that every map
begins as a blank page
and someone walking the land,
someone wondering
about the sweep of distance
and what lies between one landmark
and the next one. This is how I wondered
where you were before I found you,
and now how I look at the space
between your hand and mine
until eventually they join, two lifelines
meshing, mapping the blank spaces,
connecting heart lines,
finding our way, full of love and wonder.

VIII

When I think of you telling me
I love you,
I hear your voice spilling
as light, a pledge
that illuminates the entire sky.
Every day, all day,
I see because you light the way.
And at night, as you sleep,
I sometimes watch your eyelids flutter
with dream's activity,
and at those times, I know
that the stars quiver in the darkness
as they net the light
of your dreams.

IX

I imagine a Sunday afternoon, summer.
I imagine the earthen smell of potatoes cooking
and our fingers pink with the juice
of strawberries. And the scent of shortcake
baking, and sweet with almond oil.
A purple finch will come to our feeder.
Later, a cardinal. We will kiss,
then go on about the business
of the rest of the day, a few chores,
preparing a salad, making the bed
with clean linens that we fold back
making an envelope, open as an invitation.

X

I dreamed of my hand writing.
That is, I dreamed
of my eye following my hand
as it wrote. I saw the letters
collect into words, then gather
in my wordless palm
that earlier, as you slept, I had allowed
to slide over your hair
and down your breast
and let lodge under the side of your rib
where your heart was beating
speaking to me, softly,
of love and breath and forever.

XI

I think of water
that travels, always assured
of reaching its sea,
of rejoining its larger destiny,
despite the suckling landscape
of trees and blessed grasses,
despite the resisting rocks that always,
in good time, yield
to the waters that ache toward home.
This is how I love you,
must love you, answering your call,
as water, intent on meeting you
at the heart of my yearning.

XII

Today I thought of kisses,
which is another way
of thinking of you,
the sweet, glad heart
that kisses me from my drowsy
stupor in which I forget,
I too often forget, that I am glad,
that the dream I dream has wakened,
is alive when you kiss me,
so please kiss me. Kiss me.
O, never forget to kiss me.